HOW TO
Comfort
Someone
IN CRISIS

A Christian's Guide to Being
the Greatest Help During
a Time of Great Need

DEIDRE MARIE

How to Comfort Someone in Crisis:
A Christian's Guide to Being the Greatest Help
During a Time of Great Need

ISBN: 978-1-956701-22-7 Paperback
          978-1-956701-23-4 eBook

Publisher's Cataloging-in-Publication Data
Names: Marie, Deidre, author.
Title: How to comfort someone in crisis : a Christian's guide to being the greatest help
during a time of great need / Deidre Marie.
Description: San Diego, CA : Grace and Faith Press, 2025.
Identifiers: ISBN 978-1-956701-22-7 (paperback) | ISBN 978-1-956701-23-4 (ebook)
Subjects: LCSH: Illustrated works. | Suffering--Religious aspects--Christianity. |
Christian life. | Psychic trauma--Religious aspects--Christianity. | Consolation. |
Pastoral care. | BISAC: RELIGION / Christian Living / Inspirational. | RELIGION /
Christian Ministry / Pastoral Resources.
Classification: LCC BV4909 .D45 2025 (print) | LCC BV4909 (ebook) | DDC
259.22--dc23.

DEDICATION

To Mark and Jordan,
Thank you for reflecting God's light during my darkest days.

TABLE OF CONTENTS

HOW TO COMFORT SOMEONE IN CRISIS

PREFACE

I write this book as a woman of faith. I am neither a chaplain, a pastor, nor a counselor. During my six decades on this Earth, I have experienced the joyful heights of life's beautiful blessings, but I've also felt the painful depths of its sorrow. I've spent a lot of time in the valley. Me and the Lord.

From my own childhood trauma, my 12-year old brother's suicide, witnessing domestic violence in my home growing up, and experiencing multiple life-threatening medical conditions as an adult, including cancer, I have come to know crises on a deeply personal level. I also know it tangentially, as a loved one, relative, and close friend of others who have experienced their own crisis moments.

Through my own and my loved ones' valley experiences, God has given me a unique insight, wisdom, and ability. Much in the same way that elder college students can earn "experiential credits" toward their degree for their years of working on the job, my experiences with crisis situations have earned me expert status and credibility in knowing and understanding what suffering people need at such times.

During my times of great need and also as a church leader who has helped others in need over the years, I have seen what people do well and what they don't do so well in their desire to help, even with the best of intentions and the biggest of hearts.

So, with this book, I aim to share as much as I can about how to help someone who is experiencing a crisis. While I'm coming from a Christian perspective, the information in this book applies not only to helping a fellow Christian in crisis, but it also applies to helping a non-believer as well. Who knows, God might just be using you to show the love and light of Christ to someone for the first time, which could lead to their ultimate acceptance of a lifelong relationship with our Savior.

I pray this book will give you practical information, spiritual strength, and divine encouragement to do what God calls all believers to do—to serve and love each other as His hands and feet on earth.

God's peace be with you.

Deidre Marie

INTRODUCTION

God calls us to serve one another not only in good times, but also during times of distress. When the need is greatest, those who want to serve are not always equipped to help, nor do they feel they know how to help. They just do it. While their heart is in the right place, knowing how to help is not instinctive to everyone. Some people just know how to be there. Others are awkward, but still show up. Yet others shy away completely even though they know in their hearts they are needed.

No matter which type of person you are, you can learn how to be there for someone who is going through a crisis. I'm writing this book as someone who has both needed comforting and answered God's call to comfort others during the scary times of life.

This book is divided into four parts: In Part I, I share with you how a crisis is defined for the purposes of this book, a list of different types of crises, and how a crisis impacts the mind, body, and spirit. In Part II, I share what the Bible says about how God sees our suffering and His different roles in it.

Next, in Part III, I explain God's call to believers to comfort one another, giving you guidelines for how to respond to and support someone, as well as practical options and suggestions for doing so. In Part IV, I discuss how not to lose yourself in the process of helping and how to recognize and what to do when the needs of someone in crisis are more than what you can give.

At the end of the book, the appendix called *Quick References* gives you lists of comforting scriptures, comforting prayers, and helpful resources for supporting a person who is suffering in crisis.

In all their suffering he also suffered,
and he personally rescued them.
In his love and mercy, he redeemed them.
He lifted them up and carried them
through all the years.

~ISAIAH 63:9 NLT

PART I
UNDERSTANDING THE CRISIS
AND ITS IMPACT

CHAPTER 1
What Is a Crisis?

Getting right to the point, the Cambridge Dictionary defines a "crisis" as a time of great difficulty, danger, or suffering.[1] Sometimes the word is used to describe something awful that's happening at a level that is far removed from us personally, such as a national crisis, involving the economy or the government; or such as an international crisis, involving war between countries or groups. This type of crisis, we hear about on the news, but we are not always close enough to have it affect us on an individual level. We feel compassion, empathy, and heartache for the people involved, we pray for them, but usually, we are not in a position to do much more than that.

Other uses of the word crisis describe experiences that are not what most people would consider true emergencies, such as a midlife crisis, which is when someone is dealing with the emotional effects of their age and all that growing old entails; or as in an identity crisis that involves more psychological questioning of one's purpose and dealing with the uncertainty and confusion of their role in life. This in no way is meant to diminish the impact of a midlife or identity crisis. I cite these only to distinguish and differentiate what this book is not about.

So, for the purposes of this book, the word crisis refers to:

> *An unexpected event that disrupts a person's life or livelihood and causes them great difficulty, puts them in danger, or creates substantial suffering.*

From divorce to job loss, from a life-threatening diagnosis to the death of a loved one and its aftermath, I use the word crisis to refer to something that comes out of nowhere and feels like a can't-catch-your-breath punch in the gut. A complete and total disruption to someone's life.

While people experience crisis events and situations every day around the world, no one is ever really prepared for them. This is what makes crises so difficult, scary, and overwhelming. Not only for the person experiencing it, but also for those who care about and want to support that person.

CHAPTER 2
Types of Crisis Situations

Now that you know what a crisis is for the purposes of this book, it's important to look at the different types of crisis situations or events that people can be faced with.

Making a list of the possible types of crisis events may seem strange; however, it is important to do because it helps us face and understand the true heartbreaking nature of what someone could be experiencing. It's also important to recognize that, depending on the circumstances, the crisis can vary in its duration. It can be a short-term crisis, one that is brief and resolved quickly; a long-term crisis that can last months or years; or a crisis of indefinite nature, one that has no end in sight or is terminal. This list is by no means exhaustive, but my goal is to give you an idea of the possible scenarios of suffering that need our comfort. I organized these by broad categories, as follows:

Death of a ...
- loved one
- spouse
- child

- unborn child/miscarriage
- close friend

Victim of a …
- violent crime
- abuse
- theft
- injury
- accident
- betrayal
- natural disaster

Diagnosis of a …
- life-threatening illness
- cancer
- chronic disease

Loss of a …
- job
- spouse via divorce
- home
- relationship
- sobriety

Discovery of…
- infidelity
- lies/deceit/secret
- other violation of trust
- addiction
- eating disorder

Revelation of…
- a loved one being arrested
- a loved one going to jail
- moral mistakes of a spouse, child, or relative

Sadly, the list of potential crises can go on and on. What is important is to be able to recognize that a person is dealing with one and how it potentially is, or has been, affecting them. Sometimes, it's obvious; other times, it's more subtle or even purposefully hidden. In the next chapter, we will learn about the holistic effects of a crisis on a person's life.

HOW TO COMFORT SOMEONE IN CRISIS

CHAPTER 3
The Impact of a Crisis on Mind, Body, and Spirit

Without getting into how to help just yet, let's look at the impact a crisis event has on the whole person—the mind, body, and spirit.

The Lord created us as fully integrated beings. He created the mind, body, and spirit to work together to give us balance and a sense of wellbeing. A person's mind, or the mental and emotional part of who they are, gives us the ability to think clearly and be emotionally healthy. The body, or the physical part of a person, is a miraculous system of cellular, musculo-skeletal, and organ integration that keeps our hearts beating and enables us to see, move, and breathe. The spirit, or the life-force given to us from God, transcends body and mind, connects us to God, and gives us the ability to believe in and have faith in the unseen.

When a crisis happens, the mind-body-spirit balance and wellness are shaken to their core. A crisis affects all three parts, both separately and together.

The Mind

When a crisis happens, it throws the mind into a state of overload, confusion, and emotional shock. In the short-term, this threatens our ability to process our thoughts and make sense of what is happening all around us. The mind affected by crisis changes how it perceives sights, sounds, smells, tastes, and touch, usually as a measure of prioritizing what is most important to a person's survival.

The long-term effects, as we try to resume a normal life, can range from struggling with anxious thoughts of worry and dread to intrusive thoughts and flashbacks and disturbing visions. All of this can lead to a sense of hopelessness, depression, and other debilitating, trauma-related mental health problems.[2]

> *My thoughts trouble me and I am distraught.*
> ~Psalm 55:2 NIV

The Body

The stress and suffering that results from a crisis not only affects our minds, it affects our physical body as well. Based on the research of Bessel van der Kolk, MD, the author of *The Body Keeps the Score*, we now know that our bodies hold on to the emotions of a crisis. This means that our body's reaction to the stress—the muscle tension, the release of fight or flight hormones, and its immune system breakdown—often stays with us and is repeated as we live with the memories, flashbacks, or ongoing nature of the crisis.[3]

The physical effects, in the short term, range from sleep troubles, chest pain, tension headaches, and fatigue to heart palpitations, overall pain, and digestive problems. In the long term, these effects can lead to serious, life-threatening diseases, especially if the body is already predisposed genetically to certain illnesses, such as cancer, diabetes, and autoimmune diseases.

> *I am poured out like water, and all my bones are out of joint. My heart has turned to wax; it has melted within me. My mouth is dried up like a potsherd, and my tongue sticks to the roof of my mouth; you lay me in the dust of death.*
> ~Psalm 22:14-15 NIV

The Spirit

While the mind processes what has happened, and the body physically responds to the crisis, the spirit rushes to understand it from a faith perspective. Depending upon the person's relationship with God and their spiritual experiences, a crisis could raise questions or doubts about God's presence in their lives. This could lead to wondering why their prayers are unanswered, leaving them with feelings of abandonment or punishment by God. All of this can create a disconnect from, or apathy toward, their faith in Him and His promises. Others may feel let down by the response to their crisis, or lack thereof, from their church family or others in their faith community.

> *The Lord is close to the brokenhearted and saves those who are crushed in spirit.* ~Psalm 34:18 NIV

Crisis Effects on the Mind, Body, and Spirit in the Bible

These mind-body-spirit reactions are normal human responses to the unexpected and scary experiences that don't make earthly sense or follow human logic. Even the Bible is full of stories in both the Old and New Testaments, where God's people unravel mentally and emotionally, become physically weak, and question their faith during times of great distress.

One of the most recognizable examples of this is found in the story of Job and how he lost everyone he loved and everything important to him. The Bible is very clear about how his crisis affected mind, body, and spirit. His mind suffered with deep despair, grief, confusion, and lament. His physical body responded to the crisis with painful, disfiguring boils from head to toe. They were so awful that they caused him to scrape his skin for relief and left him unrecognizable. Spiritually, Job questioned God's actions, angrily accused God of treating him as an enemy, and even cursed the day that God allowed him to be born.[4]

Of course, David faced several crisis situations, involving betrayal of those he trusted, plots of his enemies, and the consequences of his own sin. We see in the Book of Psalms that David's mind suffered from anxiety, insomnia, and all sorts of mental torment. He wrote of how his physical body became weak and how his bones were wasting away during these times. And the Psalms themselves are filled with David's pleas to God for help and spiritual sustenance.[5]

Another example is found in the story of Hannah, the mother of the prophet Samuel. Her crisis was spread out over several years as she lived in the shame and ridicule of not being able to conceive. The ability to bear children in those days defined a woman's identity. She was so distressed by the situation that her mind was filled with bitterness, anguish, sorrow, and ultimately deep depression, as she endured taunting of those around her. Her body shut down, causing her to lose her appetite and stop eating. Her spirit was so broken that she constantly called on God to help her and grant her request for a child.[6]

Even the mind, body, and spirit of the Son of the Living God were affected by his crisis of betrayal, torture, and crucifixion. Jesus's mind was overwhelmed with anguish and sorrow, knowing what he was about to face. His body, before being beaten by Roman soldiers, began to sweat drops of blood and become weak as he realized what was about to happen to him. Spiritually, Jesus prayed and pleaded with God in the Garden of Gethsemane, and he openly cried out to God, asking why He had abandoned him as he suffered immeasurable pain on the cross.[7]

With each of these crisis stories in the Bible, we see how God shows His loving presence in their pain. Job, David, Hannah, and our Messiah Jesus all ultimately found peace in a place of acceptance and trust in the Lord.

This doesn't mean that everything always turned out as they had hoped, sometimes they did, sometimes they did not.

Either way, they knew that God was with them no matter what and that His faithfulness endures forever. And, just as the crisis affected their minds, bodies, and spirits, the power of God's presence overcame the effects and restored them.

Knowing that God will do the same for us, these examples from the Bible can help sustain today's Christian in crisis. Through their stories of challenge and despair, God shows us how important it is to trust Him during the storms of life, remembering that His ways are not our ways.

For my thoughts are not your thoughts, neither are your ways my ways," declares the Lord. As the heavens are higher than the earth, so are my ways higher than your ways and my thoughts than your thoughts. ~Isaiah 55:8-9 NIV

The Lord is close to the brokenhearted
and saves those who are crushed in spirit.

~PSALM 34:18 NIV

PART II
A GODLY PERSPECTIVE
OF OUR TIMES OF CRISIS

CHAPTER 4
How God Sees Our Suffering

With our limited human perspective from living in a broken world, we see a crisis and its suffering differently than the way God sees it.

When we believe that God has abandoned us in our suffering, He not only shows us that He is present, but He also suffers with us. Even more, He redeems us and never leaves us, making a way for us to draw closer to Him.

In all their suffering he also suffered, and he personally rescued them. In his love and mercy, he redeemed them. He lifted them up and carried them through all the years.
~Isaiah 63:9 NLT

When we don't understand why the crisis happened, God sees how it fits into His larger story of healing, redemption, power, and grace. His divine vision sees a way to use the suffering we face for His glory and our ultimate good.

And we know that all things work together for good to them that love God, to them who are the called according to his purpose.
~Romans 8:28 KJV

Where we see and feel only the pain, God sees and feels our suffering with a deeply compassionate love and an empathic heart.

Jesus wept. ~John 11:35 KJV

Many believers who have been delivered from an awful crisis, look back and see God's hand, lesson, and protection in their situation. Some see God giving them an opportunity to grow in a deeper relationship with Him. Some see God's testing of their faith and trust in Him.

In the moment, however, it may seem nearly impossible for the person suffering through a desperate, life-changing difficulty to see their situation as God does. However, for those who are supporting them, remembering God's perspective is a lifeline to hope. It gives the supporter strength to do God's work of being a light to someone in need. With God's light shining through you, you are enabled to remind them that they are not forgotten, not unseen, not alone, that they are deeply loved, tenderly held, forgiven, and fully known by the Lord.

CHAPTER 5
God's Roles in Our Time of Great Need

With His empathic heart to feel what we feel, His compassionate eyes to see our pain, His promise to use our crisis for His glory and our good, and His eternal presence, we can begin to see and accept God's many roles in our suffering. The Bible says that in our times of crisis, God is:

Our Comforter
His loving presence consoles, calms, and comforts us at our lowest moments.

> *All praise to God, the Father of our Lord Jesus Christ. God is our merciful Father and the source of all comfort.*
> ~2 Corinthians 1:3 NLT

Our Sustainer
The Lord actively supports us in all things and at all times, He helps us endure without being destroyed, He supplies us with life's necessities through the pain.

> *Cast your burden on the Lord, and he will sustain you; he will never permit the righteous to be moved.* ~Psalm 55:22 ESV

Our Guide

God's divine guidance leads, directs, and assists us in navigating the choppy waters of this earthly life with His Word and with His hearing and answering our prayers.

If any of you lacks wisdom, you should ask God, who gives generously to all without finding fault, and it will be given to you. ~James 1:5 NIV

Our Refiner

God's love for us pushes us to our limits sometimes, in order to strip away the impurities and strengthen our character and faith as believers. God refines us by deepening our roots, testing our faith, putting us through trials to reveal His glory.

Not only so, but we also glory in our sufferings, because we know that suffering produces perseverance; perseverance, character; and character, hope. ~Romans 5:3-4 NIV

Our Deliverer

God delivers us from the shackles of pain and suffering, freeing and rescuing us from the oppression, bondage, or danger of a crisis.

The righteous cry out, and the Lord hears them; he delivers them from all their troubles. ~Psalm 34:17 NIV

Our Present Help
God is fully present and actively involved at all times of a crisis. He is immediately available to hear our prayers and give us the assistance that we need during our darkest times.

God is our refuge and strength, an ever-present help in trouble.
~Psalm 46:1 NIV

Our Eternal Hope
Through His giving of His Son to die on the cross for us, through the promises and encouragement of His Word, and through the examples in the Bible of those He sustained, God is our eternal hope.

"For I know the plans I have for you," declares the Lord, "plans to prosper you and not to harm you, plans to give you hope and a future. ~Jeremiah 29:11 NIV

PART III
OBEYING GOD'S CALL
TO COMFORT EACH OTHER

CHAPTER 6
What God Calls Us to Do

What do you do when you learn of someone's crisis? Be it the death of their loved one, the loss of their job, a divorce, a cancer diagnosis, a natural disaster, or any of the infinite possible scenarios of suffering, how do you respond?

Unlike law enforcement or emergency medical personnel, who run toward the crisis, our instinct as regular people is usually to run away from it. We reason that we're not trained to help and that the people in need would be better served by the "professionals."

Many times, that is true. But for crisis situations and events like those mentioned above and in Chapter 2, the aid and support of the professional only goes so far and may not be available at all, depending on the situation. Even then, they are usually focused on resolving the immediate matter at hand, not the physical, emotional, or spiritual toll of the crisis and its aftermath.

This is where the faith community comes in. God makes it very clear what He wants during these times. No matter at what point of a crisis—before, during or after—God calls His believers to be like Him, to comfort those in need, to reflect His light and heart, and to be His hands and feet on earth.

Even *before* a crisis ever happens, we have a responsibility to each other as believers. God calls His people to:

- Love each other.
  "A new command I give you: Love one another. As I have loved you, so you must love one another. By this everyone will know that you are my disciples, if you love one another."
  ~John 13:34-35 NIV

- Serve each other.
  For you have been called to live in freedom, my brothers and sisters. But don't use your freedom to satisfy your sinful nature. Instead, use your freedom to serve one another in love.
  ~Galatians 5:13 NLT

- Be kind to each other.
  See that no one pays back evil for evil, but always try to do good to each other and to all people.
  ~1 Thessalonians 5:15 NLT

- Encourage each other.
  Let us think of ways to motivate one another to acts of love and good works. And let us not neglect our meeting together, as some people do, but encourage one another, especially now that the day of his return is drawing near.
  ~Hebrews 10:24-25 NLT

- Have fellowship with each other.
  That which we have seen and heard we proclaim also to you, so that you too may have fellowship with us; and indeed our fellowship is with the Father and with his Son Jesus Christ. ~1 John 1:3 NIV

- Confess sins and pray for each other.
  Therefore confess your sins to each other and pray for each other so that you may be healed. The prayer of a righteous person is powerful and effective. ~James 5:16 NIV

- Share the hope of the Lord.
  May the God of hope fill you with all joy and peace in believing, so that by the power of the Holy Spirit you may abound in hope. ~Romans 15:13 ESV

In addition to the above, God gives us even more instruction during times of difficulty and crisis. He specifically calls us to:

- Carry each other during hard times.
  Carry each other's burdens, and in this way you will fulfill the law of Christ. ~Galatians 6:2 NIV

- Be a friend who is near during times of distress.
  Never abandon a friend—either yours or your father's. When disaster strikes, you won't have to ask your brother for assistance. It's better to go to a neighbor than to a brother who lives far away. ~Proverbs 27:10 NLT

- Feed the hungry and help others who are in trouble.
  If you extend your soul to the hungry and satisfy the afflicted soul, then your light shall dawn in the darkness, and your darkness shall be as the noonday. ~Isaiah 58:10 NKJV

- To be there in the good times and the bad times.
  Rejoice with those who rejoice; mourn with those who mourn. ~Romans 12:15 NIV

- Comfort others the same way that God has comforted us.
  Praise be to the God and Father of our Lord Jesus Christ, the Father of compassion and the God of all comfort, who comforts us in all our troubles, so that we can comfort those in any trouble with the comfort we ourselves receive from God. ~2 Corinthians 1:3-4 NIV

Stories of Comforters in the Bible

To illustrate obedience to God's call, here are a few snapshot examples of His people comforting each other in the Bible. One example is how Ruth refused to leave the side of her mother-in-law, Naomi, after she lost her sons and everything she owned. Ruth's commitment and dedication helped Naomi get her through her despair.[8]

But Ruth replied, "Don't urge me to leave you or to turn back from you. Where you go I will go, and where you stay I will stay. Your people will be my people and your God my God. Where you die I will die, and there I will be buried. May the Lord deal with me, be it ever so severely, if even death separates you and me." ~Ruth 1:16-17 NIV

After Job lost everything and everyone he loved, his friends, Eliphaz, Bildad, and Zophar, traveled to visit with him, using their presence to comfort him. Their compassion for him was not based on actions or words even. They were there simply to love him during his time of deep trauma and despair.[9]

> *Then they sat on the ground with him for seven days and seven nights. No one said a word to him, because they saw how great his suffering was.* ~Job 2:13 NIV

Jesus cried with Martha and Mary when he found out that their brother, Lazarus, had died. Jesus felt their painful loss not only because Lazarus was Jesus' friend, but also because he was moved by their sorrow. This type of kindness and comfort was powerful because Jesus knew that he would reverse their pain when he raised Lazarus from the dead.[10]

> *When Jesus saw her weeping, and the Jews who had come along with her also weeping, he was deeply moved in spirit and troubled. Where have you laid him?" he asked. "Come and see, Lord," they replied. Jesus wept.* ~John 11:33-35 NIV

Before his reign as king, David was called to share his musical talent to soothe Saul's soul, which was tormented by evil spirits that took over him when he chose to depart from God's ways.[11]

> *Whenever the spirit from God came on Saul, David would take up his lyre and play. Then relief would come to Saul; he would feel better, and the evil spirit would leave him.* ~1 Samuel 16:23 NIV

When Jesus' disciples suffered the anxiety, grief, and uncertainty of the prospect of His leaving them and being crucified, Jesus, the comforter of all comfort, calmed their distress with beautiful words of the truth of his mission to save us, never leave us, and prepare a place in Heaven for us.[12]

> *"Do not let your hearts be troubled. You believe in God; believe also in me. My Father's house has many rooms; if that were not so, would I have told you that I am going there to prepare a place for you? And if I go and prepare a place for you, I will come back and take you to be with me that you also may be where I am. You know the way to the place where I am going."*
> ~John 14:1-4 NIV

The Apostle Paul wrote many letters to encourage and comfort early believers who, like him, faced persecution in Rome, Philippi, Thessalonica, Corinth, Ephesus, Colosse, and Galatia. These letters reflected his care and commitment to his roles as "increaser of the faith" and spreader of the Gospel to Gentiles. Paul was someone who could empathize with their struggle.[13]

> *We are hard pressed on every side, but not crushed; perplexed, but not in despair; persecuted, but not abandoned; struck down, but not destroyed. We always carry around in our body the death of Jesus, so that the life of Jesus may also be revealed in our body.* ~2 Corinthians 4:8-10 NIV

With gratitude for God's direction through scripture and the examples of people comforting each other in the Bible, we can now move on to Chapter 7, where we'll look at what specifically we can do in these days and times to carry out God's call to comfort.

CHAPTER 7
Guidelines for How to Respond and Comfort

In responding to God's call to comfort, we first must know that we are not alone. Not only is God present with those suffering during a crisis, but He's also present with us as we do the work of supporting people in the middle of one. With His Word, divine inspiration, our own previous experiences of God comforting us, and answered prayer to guide us, we can truly find the strength, courage, and peace to be like Him, as He asks of us.

In my roles as someone who needed comfort many times and as someone who has been called to give comfort, I find that the following actions are the most helpful in caring for someone:

Prepare and Lead with Prayer
When we pray, God prepares us to let the Holy Spirit lead us. This is the best way to prepare to minister to others. When we stay in prayer, the close presence and wisdom of God takes over and gives us strength and resolve. When praying,

pray for the person in crisis, pleading for God to comfort them, to relieve their burden and suffering, and to give them peace in their storm; and also pray for yourself, ask God for strength and poise.

Whenever possible, pray in the presence of the person in crisis. It's so important to pray *with* them, and not just for them. As part of the prayer time, read and share Bible verses that apply to their situation and bring comfort, not correction. If unable to pray with the person, send them a note with your prayer for them, along with helpful Bible verses. Or ask to pray with them during a phone call or a video chat, if possible.

With the person's permission, enlist the help of trusted prayer groups and other prayer warriors in your faith community, when appropriate. Ask them to join you in prayer for the person in crisis.

Before arriving to see my friend, Charlotte, who was in the hospital during the last days of her battle with cancer, I had no idea of what I would see. So, I took time to pray beforehand. I prayed alone for God's strength to be a comfort to her, despite her being unconscious, and I reached out to others in our church family to pray with me for God to relieve our sister-in-Christ of the pain she was in. By the time I arrived, God's supernatural strength came over me and enabled me to be a comfort to her and her husband as well.

For a list of Comforting Prayers for the one in crisis and the one who is called to comfort them, see the *Quick References* section on page 67.

> *Be careful for nothing; but in everything by prayer and supplication with thanksgiving let your requests be made known unto God. And the peace of God, which passeth all understanding, shall keep your hearts and minds through Christ Jesus.*
> ~Philippians 4:6-7 KJV

Be There with Empathy

This aspect of support, which means being fully present in, and attempting to understand, someone else's pain, can be a very difficult task for many people. The idea of stepping into the dark times of someone in crisis is scary and can make us uneasy. There is so much unknown about what we will see and feel when we step foot into their place of pain. But the Bible says we must be willing to be in their presence, and identify or have empathy for their suffering, even if we've never experienced what they are going through.

And if you have experienced what they are going through, your presence is even more appropriate and valuable. I experienced this firsthand with my young friend, Elena, who was diagnosed with a very aggressive form of cancer. As someone who had received my own cancer diagnosis a few years earlier, I felt that God put me in a position to be a light to her as she navigated her cancer journey, as she referred to it. I not only shared my experiences with my doctors, treatment, and nutrition, I encouraged her with specific scriptures from God's Word that helped me in my own time of weakness, pain, and uncertainty. We cried together, prayed together, and became closer in the process. I believe that her seeing me as someone who knew firsthand what she was going through gave her strength to fight and try to heal.

My experience with Elena, showed me that being there with empathy doesn't require the perfect words or the perfect prayer. The gift is you and your willingness to face them, sit with them, cry with them, and be there in their time of need.

> *Rejoice with those who rejoice and weep with them that weep.*
> ~Romans 12:15 NLT

Listen with Love

Resist the urge to give advice at this time of crisis. Whether in their presence or on a call, remember that people in crisis situations may need for you to simply listen as they vent and process. Listening with love puts the focus on them and what they actually need versus what you think they need. The act of listening with love is both healing and comforting.

I remember checking in on a widow, an older woman who lost her husband. Several weeks had passed, and she hadn't been back to church. So, we needed to make sure she was okay. As I sat with her, she talked and talked and talked some more about her husband, sometimes repeating the stories that she had already told. Sometimes, I couldn't get a word in at all. Her pain was so deep that her way of dealing with it was to express how much she missed and loved him. Her process was hers, and I believe the act of allowing her to talk was the comfort she needed at that time.

Understand this, my dear brothers and sisters: You must all be quick to listen, slow to speak, and slow to get angry.
~James 1:19 NLT

Practice Patience

As with listening with love, practicing patience allows us to learn how the person is reacting to their crisis and how they're managing their grief and processing their pain. As in all things, everyone responds differently. Some people are quiet reflectors, who seek God inwardly. Others are more vocal and emotional in their response. Still others are flat out angry and take out their anger on those of us who want to help. When facing the difficult reactions, dig deep and pray for a godly patience that knows not to take it personally. Continue to be kind and patient as they heal.

When a member of our church family found out that his daughter had a rare, incurable illness, he was angry. The man that we had come to know as kind, giving, and outgoing suddenly became short-tempered and self-absorbed. He acted this way before any of us knew about the diagnosis and what their family was facing. Once we found out, however, we were able to understand, and that enabled us compassionately to practice patience with him. We all prayed for him and his family, and some of us prayed with him, trusting that God would give him the comfort that we could not give him.

Love is patient, love is kind. It does not envy, it does not boast, it is not proud. ~1 Corinthians 13:4 NIV

Meet Them Where They Are
This aspect of support and comfort takes into consideration where a person in crisis is emotionally. Some people face the crisis in real time, having accepted the truth and reality of the situation. On the opposite extreme, others remain in denial, not ready to accept the truth, not ready to process any part of it. Most people fall somewhere in between as they seek to understand and accept their altered reality.

Either way, it is not our job to push anyone into an emotional space that they are not ready for. For example, rushing someone into talking about making funeral arrangements before they are ready. They may never be ready, needing someone else to do it. Or forcing a terminally ill patient to discuss how they feel about dying.

My friend Dolores, a fellow breast cancer patient I met during a hospital seminar on cancer treatment, knew full well that her time was limited. During our weekly conversations, I learned that she was not one to wallow in sadness. Instead, she preferred to tell jokes and funny stories so that we could have deep belly laughs together on our calls. This remained true even toward the end when her breathing began to be more labored. Our last phone conversation, a few days before her passing, was about her hospice nurse being "so serious."

She wanted to laugh and needed to laugh. Meeting her where she was emotionally—preferring laughter over lamenting—helped me give her the comfort she needed. Yes, I was so saddened by her passing, but I know that in a small yet powerful way, God enabled me to meet her where she was and give her comfort. Praise God for that!

> *Finally, be all of one mind, be loving toward one another, be gracious, and be kind.* ~1 Peter 3:8 MEV

With these guidelines in mind, we can go into even more detail about practical ways to help, as we'll see in the next chapter.

HOW TO COMFORT SOMEONE IN CRISIS

CHAPTER 8
Practical Options and Suggestions

Building on and following the guidelines in Chapter 7, we can now offer practical, thoughtful, and considerate ways to comfort someone who is in crisis, giving them a lifeline of hope when they are overwhelmed or feeling forgotten during their hardest days. Here are a few:

Arrange for a Short Visit

Don't force it, but ask to visit so that you can sit with them, listen with love, and pray with them wherever they are, at home or in the hospital. See the *Quick References* section on page 71 for the list of Comforting Prayers to pray with someone going through a time of hardship. There is nothing like being in someone's presence, holding their hands, and taking up space with them. Preferably in person, but a virtual video visit is the next best thing.

When I was in the hospital after suffering a pulmonary embolism near the end of my son's senior year in high school, I was so touched to receive visitors who lovingly sat with me and prayed right there in my room. Not just my friends, but the parents of my son's friends as well. I believe their prayers helped me heal from that painful medical situation and enabled me miraculously to attend my son's high school graduation a few weeks later.

Offer to Help with Tasks

The everyday tasks of life often pile up during a crisis. You can offer to run errands, baby sit, pet sit, make meals, arrange for meal trains, do housework, buy groceries, give rides, make phone calls, go with them to doctor or other appointments, do administrative tasks, like pay bills or schedule appointments, just to name a few.

Try to be specific when you offer to help, but if you don't have any idea of what they might need help with, simply ask, "How can I bless you today?" I did this with my friend, Vicky, who was being treated for stage four cancer. Before her surgery, I cooked several meals to put in her freezer, knowing she would need healthy food as she recovered at home. As time went on, I asked how I could bless her, and to my surprise, she asked me to accompany her to her appointment with her oncologist because no one in her family could go with her. I didn't know she needed that, and I'm so glad that I offered. You don't always know what someone needs, so offering to be a blessing opens the door to finding out.

Send Notes, Letters, and Messages of Love

Handwritten notes, greeting cards, or well-worded texts can be a really great way to share comforting words of God's truth and give much-needed encouragement.

This is true even if the person in crisis is someone in your community that you don't know directly. One morning, I read a newspaper article about a 12-year-old boy who committed suicide, leaving his family, especially his mother, in complete shock and devastation. I did not know the family, and I wasn't sure if they were Christian or not. Still, I felt compelled to send a letter to the boy's mother. I told her about how my family had been in the same situation many years before, when my 12-year-old brother took his own life, too. I told her that my reason for writing to her was to give her hope that she and her family, with God's help, could find a way to get through this. My mother, sister, and I, by God's grace did, and so could they.

I had no idea how my letter would be received, but a few weeks later, the mother wrote back to me, thanking me for reaching out to her. She said she keeps my letter with her at all times and refers to it when she feels like she can't go on. I was so grateful that I obeyed God's call to comfort a hurting stranger in a way that only I could because of my history with a similar situation.

Another example to share from my life is what happened after I was hospitalized and released from an episode of pre-term labor at 21 weeks into my pregnancy with my son. During my eight-day hospital stay, the doctors put me through many tests, including several ultrasounds that showed me for the first time that he was a boy. At that time, I was in no position to ask for the images of my developing baby. Yet, one day at home after being released and placed on bedrest, I received a sweet letter from a nurse, who kindly took the time to send me several ultrasound pictures of my son. Her note and kind gesture comforted me and gave me hope as I carried out the rest of my pregnancy in bed. I still have that letter and ultrasound photos to this day, 34 years later.

Give Helpful Gifts
Consider giving the person in crisis a sincere and helpful gift that inspires them to feel connected to God during their time of need. You don't have to spend much to show your support. A few examples of helpful gifts include:

- A book or devotional specifically about managing or healing from the type of crisis that they're going through. For the husband of a dear friend from church, who passed away after a long battle with cancer, I found and gave him the perfect devotional about comforting the grieving spouse. He told me how he cherished that book and how it helped him through the first raw weeks of living without her.

- A gift basket or gift bag that will help make their life a little easier. This can be food, toiletries, etc. When I learn of someone receiving a cancer diagnosis, I create a gift bag with cancer prayer books and devotionals, and cancer treatment recipe books. The same can be done for any type of crisis situation.

- A blank journal for writing thoughts and prayers and processing emotions. I make scripture art that I put on the cover of blank journals. I keep them on hand and give them out to family and friends who could benefit from seeing God's Word on the cover and be inspired to speak to Him through writing in the journal.

- An album or CD with uplifting and encouraging worship music. Calming music that reminds us of God's loving presence is the perfect gift for someone going through difficult times, much like the way David's music soothed Saul's tormented soul in the Book of 1 Samuel in the Bible.[14]

Stay in Touch and Follow Up Over Time

Once the crisis is over or at least settled down a bit, there is still a lot of healing that needs to happen. This is especially true when anniversaries, birthdays, Christmas, or other meaningful dates and holidays approach that would trigger the pain of the crisis all over again. Knowing that you remember helps the person to feel loved and not so alone.

Ever since the passing of my dear friend, Elena, I send heavenly birthday wishes to her sister and mother on my friend's birthday. I know they are missing her extra on that day of the year, so my way of comforting them is to let them know that I know what day it is.

These practical options and suggestions are just a few examples that you can start with. Trust that God will lead you to the best ways, within your reach, to touch the heart of someone suffering.

Next, in Chapters 9 and 10, we'll look at what to do when the person you're supporting in crisis needs more than you're able to give and how not to lose yourself in the process of helping.

Trust in the Lord with all your heart,
and lean not on your own understanding.
In all your ways acknowledge Him,
and He shall direct your paths.

~PROVERBS 3:5-6 NKJV

PART IV
DISCERNING THE NEED
FOR MORE SUPPORT

CHAPTER 9
When They Need More Than You Can Give

There's nothing more satisfying than knowing that your acts of comfort made a difference in someone's life. Helping someone ride out, overcome, or just simply survive their crisis event shows them the love, grace, and mercy of God through you, His servant.

Sometimes, though, despite our best efforts to be the hands and feet of God on earth, we aren't always equipped to provide all the support and care that a person in crisis needs. Sometimes, they're inconsolable. Sometimes, they give up and don't think they can go on. In cases like this, we need first to be able to recognize that we can't do it all; and second, we must pray to God for guidance in directing them to the resources that are most appropriate for their situation.

Often, our instinct is to try harder to comfort, but the most loving and faithful thing you can do is to help them receive a deeper level of care that God desires for them. Your comforting care is not diminished in any way by referring them to resources and experts who are more equipped and trained specifically to handle their needs in the best and most effective way.

Depending on the situation, you may start out giving the person articles and links to online information about their crisis. (See Helpful Resources on page 76 in the *Quick References* section.) You may also mention how a Christian counselor or therapist can help with their mental health; how a pastor or spiritual advisor at church can help them address their spiritual health needs; how a support group can be helpful for their specific type of crisis, such as addiction relapse, grief, trauma, etc.; and how going to their doctor or other medical practitioner can help with their body's physical response to the stress of the situation.

Granted, this is a delicate balance that not everyone is comfortable in talking about or suggesting, but remembering God's call can give us the courage to take a small step in that direction. If they respond well or not, you know that you have done your best to lead them to the help they need.

CHAPTER 10
How Not to Lose Yourself in the Process

In line with referring the person in crisis to additional help that you are unequipped to provide, an often-overlooked aspect of supporting someone in crisis is the risk of burning out or losing oneself in the process. As someone who feels called to support others in crisis, I have found myself consumed by others' pain in an unhealthy way. By that I mean, I began feeling like my actions could save that person somehow, so much so that I exhausted myself in trying. The physical and emotional toll was so heavy that I would just shut down and not be able to help at all. Taking a break and asking for God's guidance, I learned ways to reframe my situation to remember these important facts about helping someone in crisis without being totally consumed by it:

- Always, always, always anchor yourself in Christ before you begin helping someone. As stated in Chapter 7, praying to prepare to serve is an important and best way to begin. And, as part of that, if you're prone to get too involved or too attached to a situation, you must be continually refueling and staying in touch with the Lord as you serve. Staying tethered to Him and His Word, we remember that He is the source of our ability to be there for someone in need.

I am the vine; you are the branches. If you remain in me and I in you, you will bear much fruit; apart from me you can do nothing. ~John 15:5 NIV

- Remember that only God can heal and rescue the suffering soul—not you. It is *not* your responsibility. Your job is to point the person in crisis to Jesus and reflect His loving faithfulness. He alone is the Savior, and He alone is all that the Bible says of Him.

… and his name shall be called Wonderful, Counsellor, The mighty God, The everlasting Father, The Prince of Peace… ~Isaiah 9:6 KJV

- Establish and maintain healthy boundaries in order to protect your ability to help. This means not allowing your own emotional, mental, physical, and spiritual needs to go unnurtured as you help someone else. The best way to look at it is to remember that boundaries are not barriers to loving someone, they're actually what sustains us and our ability to do so.

The prudent see danger and take refuge, but the simple keep going and pay the penalty. ~Proverbs 22:3 NIV

- Know that you are not here to help everyone. Not every cry for help, not every crisis is assigned to you. When you're unsure when or if you should become involved, ask God what part, if any part, He wants you to accept. Discerning how and when to help takes the pressure off of us to be all things to all people in need. God calls all of us believers to help, not just a few, and certainly not just you.

  We have different gifts, according to the grace that is given us.
  ~Romans 12:6 NIV

- Give support and coordinate your efforts with your faith community or church family as you serve. Many times, you're not the only one giving support to someone who is in crisis. When you know of someone else who is involved, lean on each other and work together whenever possible. If you are the only one helping, then let trusted friends or family know what you're doing. Not to brag or say, 'look at me, I'm so helpful.' No, do this to keep yourself from being isolated. You will need people to check on you, hold you up, and speak truth to you as you serve.

  Two are better than one, because they have a good return for their labor: If either of them falls down, one can help the other up. But pity anyone who falls and has no one to help them up.
  ~Ecclesiastes 4:9-10 NIV

- Try to be aware of the warning signs of losing yourself in supporting someone else. These include feeling anxious or guilty about what the other person is going through;

neglecting your own health, wellbeing, and/or responsibilities; or feeling like you can't step away, even temporarily, without fear that they will fall apart. This is when you should take a break to care for yourself.

Then, because so many people were coming and going that they did not even have a chance to eat, he said to them, "Come with me by yourselves to a quiet place and get some rest." ~Mark 6:31 NIV

- Finally, know that loving and serving someone in crisis includes letting go and letting God. When or if you see that it is time to surrender and release yourself from the crisis situation, you can do so with God's blessings, especially if you see that they are leaning on you more than on God. Or, if they push you away. Or, best case scenario, you feel they are now able to stand on their own. Of course, you will continue praying for them. But let God take the reins and do what only He can do. Trust that God's presence is not dependent on yours.

Trust in the Lord with all your heart and lean not on your own understanding. ~Proverbs 3:5 NIV

CONCLUSION

As with all times in human history, life is difficult, and suffering abounds in our broken world. No matter a person's social status, wealth, health, or other position, we all go through crisis situations that hit us with a force that can take our breath away and threaten our very way of life. During those times, believers are called to be a light in the darkness. Not only for those we love and know, but also for those who the Lord presents to us in His way and time.

When we work to see those in pain the way God does, we also find the strength to be a blessing to someone in desperate need of the Lord's light in their crisis. I pray that this book has given you enough guidance, inspiration, and tools to do just that, knowing that you don't have to be a counselor, pastor, or other professional to answer God's call to serve, to be His hands and feet on earth, and to help carry one another's burdens.

May God's light shine on you and through you.

HOW TO COMFORT SOMEONE IN CRISIS

ENDNOTES

1 "Crisis" Cambridge Dictionary, Cambridge University Press, accessed 1 July 2025. https://dictionary.cambridge.org/us/dictionary/english/crisis.

2 "Understanding the Stress Response: Chronic Activation of This Survival Mechanism Impairs Health." Harvard Health Publishing, Harvard Medical School, 3 April 2024.Web. 29 June 2025.

3 Bessel van der Kolk, M.D. *The Body Keeps the Score: Brain, Mind, and Body in the Healing of Trauma.* (New York: Penquin Books, 2015)

4 Job 1:1-42:16 (New International Version).

5 Psalms 1:1-150:6.

6 1 Samuel 1:1-2:34.

7 Matthew 26:1-27:66, Mark 14:1-15:47, Luke 22:1-23:56.

8 Ruth 1:16-17.

9 Job 2:13.

10 John 11:33-35.

11 1 Samuel 16:23.

12 John 14:1-11.

13 2 Corinthians 4:8-10.

14 1 Samuel 16:23.

APPENDIX
Quick References

<u>Comforting Scriptures</u>

These scriptures are divided by category and all reflect God's deep and abiding love for us, especially those who are walking through a time of crisis.

About God's Presence:

The Lord is close to the brokenhearted and saves those who are crushed in spirit. ~Psalm 34:18 NIV

When you pass through the waters, I will be with you and when you pass through the rivers, they will not sweep over you. ~Isaiah 43:2 NIV

Even though I walk through the valley of the shadow of death, I will fear no evil, for you are with me.
~Psalm 23:4 MEV

Be still, and know that I am God. ~Psalm 46:10 KJV

... Never will I leave you; never will I forsake you.
~Hebrews 13:5 NIV

And surely I am with you always, even to the end of the age. ~Matthew 28:20 NIV

About God's Peace:

Peace I leave with you. My peace I give to you. Not as the world gives do I give to you. Let not your heart be troubled, neither let it be afraid. ~John 14:27 MEV

You will keep in perfect peace those whose minds are stead-fast, because they trust in you. ~Isaiah 26:3 NIV

Cast all your anxiety on Him because He cares for you.
~1 Peter 5:7 NIV

About God's Strength:

But he said to me, "My grace is sufficient for you, for my power is made perfect in weakness." There for I will boast all the more gladly about my weaknesses, so that Christ's power may rest on me. ~2 Corinthians 12:9 NIV

He gives power to the weak and strength to the powerless.
~Isaiah 40:29 NLT

God is our refuge and strength, an ever-present help in trouble. ~Psalm 46:1 NIV

The Lord will fight for you, while you hold your peace."
~Exodus 14:14 MEV

Come to me, all you who are weary and burdened, and I
will give you rest. ~Matthew 11:28 NIV

My flesh and my heart may fail, but God is the strength of
my heart and my portion forever." ~Psalm 73:26 NIV

About God's Hope:

For I consider that the sufferings of this present time are
not worthy to be compared with the glory which shall be
revealed to us. ~Romans 8:18 MEV

...weeping may stay for the night, but rejoicing comes in the
morning. ~Psalm 30:5 NIV

For I know the plans I have for you," declares the Lord,
"plans to prosper you and not to harm you, plans to give
you hope and a future. ~Jeremiah 29:11 NKJV

They said to each other, "Did not our hearts burn within us
while He talked to us on the way and while He opened the
Scriptures to us?" ~Luke 24:32 MEV

About God's Listening:

... and call on me in the day of trouble; I will deliver you,
and you will honor me. ~Psalm 50:15 NIV

The righteous cry out, and the Lord hears them; He delivers them from all their troubles. ~Psalm 34:17 NIV

But in my distress I cried out to the Lord; yes, I prayed to my God for help. He heard me from his sanctuary; my cry to him reached his ears. ~Psalm 18:6 NLT

About God's Restoration:

But after you have suffered a little while, the God of all grace, who has called us to His eternal glory through Christ Jesus, will restore, support, strengthen, and establish you. ~1 Peter 5:10 MEV

He heals the brokenhearted and binds up their wounds. ~Psalm 147:3 NIV

And I will restore to you the years that the locust hath eaten, the cankerworm, and the caterpiller, and the palmerworm, my great army which I sent among you. ~Joel 2:25 KJV

The unfolding of Your words gives light; it gives understanding to the simple. ~Psalm 119:130 NIV

Blessed are those who mourn, for they will be comforted. ~Matthew 5:4 MEV

He restores my soul.... ~Psalm 23:3 NKJV

Comforting Prayers

For the Hurting

These prayers are for the person in crisis to pray; or for the supporter to pray with them, substituting the "I" and "me" with the name of the person.

I Know the Lord Sees Me and Loves Me
Dear God,
Sometimes I feel like no one sees me,
not the depth of my hurt,
not the heaviness of my burdens.
But You see me, dear Lord.
You see my quiet struggles,
You see my tears that fall in the night,
You know the ache I feel that words cannot describe.
Thank You, Lord, for not looking away.
Thank You, God, for your empathy for my pain.
Thank You, Father, for being with me and providing Your light in my darkest places.
Because of You, I know that I am not alone.
Please continue to help me trust that my suffering matters to You.
Please keep me steady when I feel like I cannot go on.
And please remind me that you fully see me and fully love me—especially when the days and nights are just too hard.
In Jesus' name, Amen.

In the Middle of My Storm
Dear God,
In the middle of this
stormy time in my life,
I come to You.
Not with any answers, and not with perfect faith,
I come to You with an open heart that longs to be near.
I need your strength when I am weak.
I need your peace when my world feels out of control.
I need your hope when the darkness creeps in.
I wish I understood why this is happening,
but I choose to trust that You are with me
even in the confusion.
The Bible says that You are near to the brokenhearted,
and today, I ask You to be near to me.
Teach me, not with shame, but with love.
Guide me, not through fear, but through grace.
And help me to see that even now,
You are holding me.
I choose to rest in Your promise that You will never
leave me, nor forsake me.
So I will keep going, making my way through
this storm, knowing and trusting You are walking
with me and lighting my way.
In Jesus' name, Amen.

While I Wait, I Will Trust

Dear God,

Sometimes, I just don't understand
Your ways or Your timing.
Sometimes, I can't hear you and the silence
feels like You are absent,
and the waiting feels like You have abandoned me.
But when I seek You, I know better.
I feel You and know that You, my God, are never late,
and never far.
So, I choose to wait and to trust,
not with bitterness, but with a bold faith.
Not with clenched fists, but with open hands.
Dear Lord, please renew my strength when I grow weary.
Please steady my heart when doubt creeps in,
and remind me that the waiting isn't wasted.
You are working even now.
Help me, please dear God, to wait for You
and trust in You, and to believe that
Your timing is perfect,
and Your love for me is unshakable.
When I cannot see my way through,
please just let me see You.
In Jesus' name, Amen.

For the Helpers

My Support for Others is Rooted in You
Dear Lord,
I surrender the urge to fix what only You can heal.
Anchor me in Your love and truth.
Show me how to help while remembering that
You alone know what is best for the hurting soul.
Please help me listen well, love gently, and let go freely.
Keep me rooted in You so that I can support others in
their time of need, not carry them.
In Jesus' name I pray, Amen.

Use Me, Lord to Comfort Someone
Dear God,
When I see that another person is hurting,
Please help me to respond like You would,
with compassion, a gentle spirit, kindness, and grace.
Remind me not to try to fix what only You can.
Please help me to be a person's safe place,
where they feel seen, heard, and loved by a
patient and faithful friend.
Please help me to reflect Your love in
every gesture, every word, every silence shared.
Teach me to share in their burdens well,
not out of obligation, but out of Your love.
And when I don't know what to say,

please help me to simply show up and be present.
Because sometimes, that is enough.
Use me, Lord, to bring comfort where there is pain,
and light where there is darkness.
Let others see Your light in me.
In Jesus' name, Amen.

Teach Me to Comfort and Love Wisely
Dear Father God,
You have called me to comfort and love others,
but not to lose myself in the trying.
You have called me to lighten someone's burdens,
but not to take on more than You ask of me.
Please give me the wisdom to know when to get involved,
and the peace to take time off when I need to rest.
Give me the strength, dear God, to love from
a place of wholeness, not depletion.
Please direct me to serve without striving, and to care
without carrying what is too heavy for me.
I surrender to You the need to be the hero, and trust
You to be the healing hero in their life, as only You can.
Please teach me holy boundaries, and show me how to
honor both compassion and rest.
In Jesus' name I pray, Amen.

Helpful Resources

General Mental Health Crisis Support

Christians In Crisis Hotline
A national, telephone-based listening and referral service staffed by trained volunteers. Offers spiritual and emotional support for those in crisis. Call 1-844-472-9687
www.christiansncrisis.com

Faithful Counseling
An online therapy platform connecting individuals to licensed Christian counselors across the U.S. Offers sliding-scale fees and integrates biblical faith.
www.faithfulcounseling.com

The Hope Line
A free, Christian peer support and crisis hotline offering counseling and referrals for emotional distress, depression, or suicidal thoughts.
www.thehopeline.com

Focus on the Family Counseling
Offers free phone consults with licensed or pastoral counselors, plus a national directory for Christian mental health and pastoral care referrals. Free one-time consult with licensed Christian counselors. Focus on the Family Counseling Line: 1-855-771-HELP (4357)
www.focusonthefamily.com/get-help/counseling-services-and-referrals/

Living Hope Ministries
Online support for individuals and family members that is
biblically grounded. www.livehope.org

Fresh Hope / Mental Health Grace Alliance
Peer-led support networks offering Christian-based support
groups for individuals and loved ones dealing with mental
health diagnoses.
www.mentalhealthgracealliance.org

National Suicide & Crisis Lifeline
A 24-hour, seven-days-a-week hotline for crisis help, where
you can ask for a faith-based counselor. Call or text 988
https://988lifeline.org/

Solihten Institute
Operates a nationwide network of faith-based counseling
centers offering integrated mind-body-spirit therapy. Accred-
ited, subsidized care aligned with Christian values.
https://solihten.org

For Grief & Loss

GriefShare
Nationwide support groups for those grieving the loss of
a loved one. Facilitated through local churches with video
teaching and group discussion guides.
www.griefshare.org

For Cancer and Chronic Illnesses

Cancer Companions
Provider of resources for cancer patients, including Bible studies, prayer partners, tools, and materials to help them cope with the challenges of cancer and its treatment.
www.cancercompanion.org

Christians Battling Cancer
An online community centered in Christ that supports, encourages, and prays for patients battling cancer.
www.christiansbattlingcancer.org

Chronic Joy Ministries
An online resource that compassionately serves people who are affected by chronic illness, mental illness, chronic pain, and disability by providing easy-to-use and accessible, faith-based educational resources and publications.
www.chronic-joy.org

For Addiction Recovery

Celebrate Recovery
A Christ-centered 12-step recovery program hosted by local churches across all 50 states. Supports recovery from addiction, pain, trauma, and life-controlling issues.
https://celebraterecovery.com

Alcoholics Anonymous
One of the original 12-step programs for healing from alcoholism and other addictions. Not Christ-centered, but many meetings take place in churches.
www.aa.org

For Trauma and Abuse

Hope for the Heart
Grace-oriented care ministries that help individuals process trauma, abuse, betrayal, and crisis through storytelling and biblical healing.
www.hopefortheheart.org

Restoration Place Counseling
Offers Christian trauma care counseling, both clinical and biblical, for women. Offering online options for receiving care.
https://rpcounseling.org

National Domestic Violence Hotline
You can request Christian counselors or advocates.
1-800-799-SAFE (7233) and www.thehotline.org

Rape, Abuse & Incest National Network (RAINN)
Request Christian or faith-based help. Call
1-800-656-HOPE (4673)
www.rainn.org

For Betrayal and Deceit

Affair Recovery
Faith-based healing programs for betrayed spouses and others.
www.affairrecovery.com

The Betrayal Trauma Recovery Podcast
Support from a Christian worldview for those navigating gaslighting and emotional abuse.
https://www.btr.org/podcast/

For Incarcerated Loved Ones and Families

Prison Fellowship
In addition to advocating for the health and wellbeing of incarcerated people, Prison Fellowship, based in biblical principles, offers care to their families to help strengthen their bond while separated by prison bars.
www.prisonfellowship.org

Crossroads Prison Ministries
Connecting those on the outside with those in prison with Bible correspondence and mentorship programs.
https://cpministries.org

For Eating Disorders

National Association of Anorexia Nervosa and Associated Disorders
A secular (non-faith-based) organization that provides free support services to anyone struggling with an eating disorder.
https://anad.org

Community Support Systems

MealTrain
A website that helps you organize meal trains, or assignments to prepare meals, for someone in need in your community.
www.mealtrain.com

Sign Up Genius
A website that helps the helpers to organize events and coordinate volunteers in the care of people in need and crisis within their faith community.
www.signupgenius.com

Applications (Apps) for Computer and Cell Phone

YouVersion Bible
This app contains 1,200+ versions of the Bible in over 2,300 languages. Search their Bible reading plans for scriptures related to specific types of crisis situations.
www.Bible.com or www.youversion.com

Abide
An app containing Christian meditations for sleep and rest.
https://abide.com

Lectio 365
Daily devotionals and scripture-based prayer app inspired by the ancient practice of Lectio Divina or divine reading.
https://www.24-7prayer.com/resource/lectio-365/

Pray As You Go
A Christian app that offers short, reflective daily guided prayers for free.
https://prayasyougo.org

SoulSpace
This app offers gentle Christian prayers and meditations for healing emotional wounds and calming the spirit.
https://soulspace.co

Dwell Bible
Audio Bible app that reads scripture with peaceful music in the background.
https://dwellapp.io

Hallow
A Christian Catholic-based prayer and meditation app with a huge variety of guided sessions of prayer, scripture readings, challenges, and Bible stories. Many celebrities take part in the readings.
https://hallow.com

These organizations and their associated website listings are current at the time of the publication of this book. However, because there might be changes to this list, I keep an up-to-date version on my website at this link:

https://deidremarie.com/christian-crisis-resources

Carry each other's burdens and in this way, you will fulfill the law of Christ.

~GALATIANS 6:2 NIV

HOW TO COMFORT SOMEONE IN CRISIS

ABOUT THE AUTHOR

A faithful believer, author, artist, and health advocate, Deidre Marie has a heart for taking care of others.

As a survivor of childhood trauma, the suicide of her 12-year-old brother, breast cancer, and other medical challenges, her artwork and writing focus on themes of faith, inspiration, encouragement, and healing. "My goal," she says, "is to bring joy and comfort to everyone who experiences my work." That work also includes speaking on topics such as breast cancer and suicide prevention.

Deidre holds a Bachelor of Science degree in Business Management from the University of Maryland and a Master of Arts degree in Communication from The American University in Washington, DC. She and her husband are empty nesters living a blessed life in San Diego, California, where they serve in leadership positions at their local church. She currently maintains a blog at www.deidremarie.com.

For More Inspiration, Follow Us At:

@graceandfaithpress on Instagram

@graceandfaithpress on Pinterest

www.graceandfaithpress.com

HOW TO COMFORT SOMEONE IN CRISIS

NOTE FROM THE PUBLISHER

Thank you so much for purchasing this book. Please reach out and let us know what you think of it and if it has been a help to you. If you feel we have left out something important, we want to know that as well. Please send your comments via email to *hello@graceandfaithpress.com*. We appreciate your thoughts and feedback, and we look forward to reading what you have to say.

Thank you!

Blessings from

www.graceandfaithpress.com